CLASSROOM TO CAREER

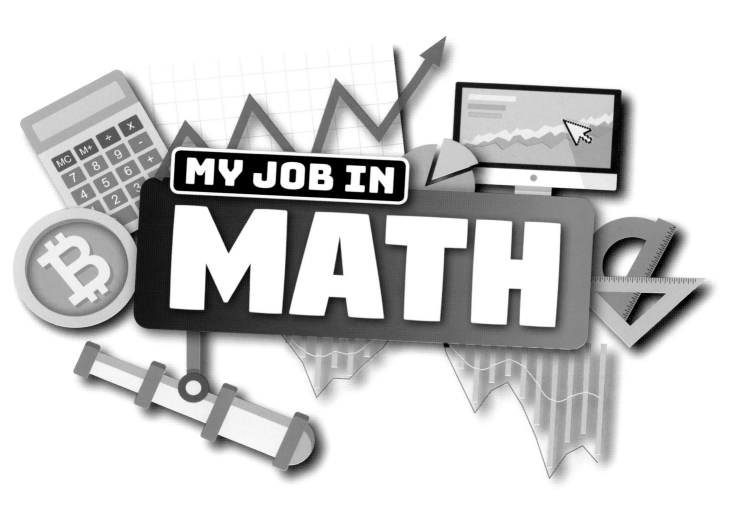

MY JOB IN

MATH

BY
JOANNA BRUNDLE

PowerKiDS
press ™

New York

Published in 2022 by The Rosen
Publishing Group, Inc.
29 East 21st Street, New York, NY 10010

© 2022 Booklife Publishing
This edition is published by arrangement
with Booklife Publishing·

Edited by:
John Wood

Designed by:
Drue Rintoul

Cataloging-in-Publication Data
Names: Brundle, Joanna.
Title: My job in math / Joanna
Brundle.
Description: New York : PowerKids
Press, 2022. | Series: Classroom to
career | Includes glossary and index.
Identifiers: ISBN 9781725336421 (pbk.)
| ISBN 9781725336445 (library bound)
| ISBN 9781725336438 (6 pack) | ISBN
9781725336452 (ebook)
Subjects: LCSH: Mathematics--
Vocational guidance--Juvenile
literature.
Classification: LCC QA10.5 B767 2022
| DDC 510.23--dc23

Manufactured in the United
States of America

CPSIA Compliance Information: Batch #CWPK22.
For Further Information contact Rosen Publishing,
New York, New York at 1-800-237-9932.

Find us on

CONTENTS

WORDS THAT LOOK LIKE THIS CAN BE FOUND IN THE GLOSSARY ON PAGE 31.

At school, your busy day is packed full of different lessons. Some of the most important are STEM subjects. Do you know what they are? STEM stands for science, technology, engineering, and math. So why are STEM subjects so important?

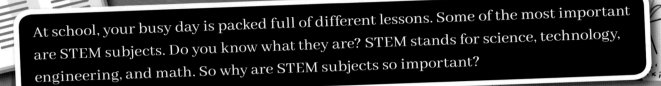

USING STEM

The world moves very fast and it changes all the time. However, STEM can help us understand it. STEM subjects can inspire you to learn more things about how the world works, and they might lead to you working in STEM. Lots of new STEM jobs are being created all the time and in lots of different areas. Who knows what you could be doing in the future? As well as helping you to find interesting work, studying STEM subjects will also help you to solve problems, make decisions, and work as part of a team.

JOB OR CAREER?

A job is something that you do to earn money. Many people stay in jobs for a short amount of time, and they don't always need training. A career is a lifelong work journey in an area that really interests you. People often need the right training for the right career.

Being a <u>university professor</u> can be a lifelong career.

STEM subjects can help you get into an exciting career, whether you want to be an astronaut, doctor, or someone who makes video games. But remember that STEM subjects are important whatever you do. For example, many careers need you to have computer skills. In this book, we are going to look at math and the careers it might lead you to. We will be thinking about how you might spend your day and what qualifications and skills you might need.

People use math every day, for example when they work out how much money things will be.

PILOT

Do you like the idea of flying around the world in an airplane or helicopter? If so, a career as a pilot could be for you. It is challenging and exciting work.

Airline pilots fly passengers and <u>cargo</u> to places all around the world. You might work for a travel company, taking tourists on vacation. You might also work for a cargo airline transporting goods such as food. If you become a military pilot, you might fly transport aircraft, taking soldiers and equipment where they are needed. As a helicopter pilot, your work might involve moving troops and important equipment in battle zones.

Fast jet pilot

Before taking off, pilots have to study weather reports to check for strong winds, thunderstorms, low clouds, and fog. They decide how much fuel is needed, check that the aircraft is safe to fly, and work out how much speed is needed to take off.

People's lives will depend on your flying skills. In order to be accepted for pilot training, you will need to be healthy and fit. A <u>degree</u> in math or <u>aviation</u> is helpful. If you are accepted, you will take written tests and flight tests. Written tests, called ground exams, cover things such as <u>navigation</u>, flight planning, and the laws of flying. In a flight test, you will need to complete many hours of flying. You will learn how to deal with emergencies, such as engine failure, by using a flight simulator. You will work as part of a team, so you will need good people skills. You will also need to be good at math and problem solving.

One of the best parts of being a pilot is traveling to different places all around the world. You may have free time to explore and relax.

Flight simulators use computers and machines to help people learn how to fly without leaving the ground.

PASSPORT

CERTIFIED PUBLIC ACCOUNTANT

Certified public accountants (CPAs) help businesses make as much money as possible. As an accountant, you might give advice, carry out <u>audits</u>, deal with <u>taxation,</u> and prepare information about people's <u>accounts</u>. Forensic accountants are specially trained to audit records to help solve crimes involving with money. They may have to show what they have found in court.

Certified public accountants can work for employers of all sizes, from large companies to small accounting businesses. An experienced accountant may become a partner (part owner of the business) or may set up a new business of their own. Accountants might also work for governments or charities.

In order to become a CPA, you will need to pass a lot of exams. These are usually taken while you are working for an accounting practice as well, so you must be interested in studying. Training usually lasts between three and five years.

You will need to be good at talking to the people you are helping. Computer skills are also important. You must also be trustworthy because you are working with people's money.

Certified public accountants usually work in an office, but you might have to visit clients to do some of the audit work. Some accounting companies will give you the chance to live in all sorts of cities around the world. It could be worth learning different languages as accountants with this extra skill are often needed.

ACOUSTIC CONSULTANT

Do you love music? Would you enjoy working in a recording studio? This is just one of the exciting roles that you might take on as an acoustic consultant.

Recording studio

Acoustic consultants think about how sound affects people and try to control it. You might check the levels of noise in a place and how well the buildings <u>absorb</u> noise. You could work on radio or television programs or appear as an expert <u>witness</u>, giving facts and opinions in court. Some acoustic consultants work at events such as music festivals. They are in charge of checking that noise levels are not too high. Some consultants give advice on how some buildings should be made, such as churches or theaters. Others work on roads and airport runways, to make sure that they follow the government's rules on how much noise can be made.

Sound travels clearly in buildings such as this concert hall. This is important for people who want to enjoy the music.

Your working day is likely to be split between an office and on-site working. There are plenty of chances to work in another country, especially if you know how to speak other languages. Acoustic consultants work for all sorts of employers. These include companies involved with building, engineering, and technology. You could also work for governments or <u>environmental organizations</u>.

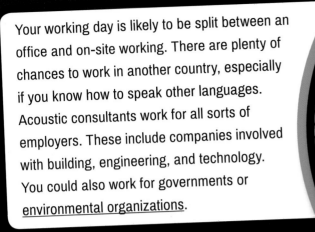

An acoustic consultant has helped to design this road, which absorbs road noise.

You could get work experience at a music festival, working for an acoustic consulting company to check noise levels.

In order to get started in this career, you will need a degree in math or a specialist subject such as audio engineering. You will also need <u>project management</u> skills. Employers will expect you to have the right work experience. Excellent IT skills are important, as acoustic consultants use noise modeling <u>software</u> in design and testing, to check how changes in design affect sound levels and quality. You will also need to understand the laws relating to noise levels.

ACTUARY

Risk is any situation involving the possibility of danger. Without realizing it, you think about risk every day – for example, deciding if it is safe to cross the road. Actuaries think about and give advice on risk involving money, particularly risks that might affect <u>insurance</u> and <u>pension</u> companies.

If you decide on a career as an actuary, you will work out the chances (known as the probability) of uncertain future events happening. You will be using your skills in math, <u>statistics,</u> and <u>economics</u> to help you do this. You will work out ways to reduce the chances of bad events happening and to cut down the costs of events that do happen.

There are many different places to work as an actuary. Possible employers include banks, <u>investment</u> <u>companies</u>, hospitals, and governments. You might work for a large company dealing with pension arrangements for its staff. You are likely to work with IT specialists to design and develop systems that follow insurance and pension laws.

Studying information is an important part of the work of an actuary.

Day to day, you will often be working out insurance rates. The insurance rate is how much people pay. Actuaries need to keep insurance rates low so that people don't have to pay too much. Actuaries also need to make sure that the rates are high enough so that if an accident does happen, there is enough money to pay for it.

Actuaries might work for car insurers. Car insurers pay for people's car accidents.

A lot of people want to be actuaries. You will need a degree in math or a similar subject, such as business or risk management. You will also have to pass a set of exams on insurance and probability. As you will be working at the same time as studying, you will need to be determined. To work in this career, you will also need to be good at explaining complicated things to people. Many people don't know about insurance, and you will have to explain it in a simple way.

MATH TEACHER

Are you mad for math? Do you like the idea of helping other young people learn? If so, why not become a math teacher?

Math is taught to students of every age, from preschools to universities. Many adults also take classes to improve their math skills. We all use math throughout our lives, whether we are checking a bill, following a recipe, or saving up for something. Math is such an important part of our lives, and that makes teaching math a rewarding career.

As a math teacher, you will plan and teach lessons to students of different ages and abilities. You will give and grade homework and prepare students to pass exams. You will have to make sure that you always keep records of your students' progress.

An important part of the role is to make sure your students have understood the lesson. Some students find math difficult, so you will need to explore different ways of keeping them interested. People learn in different ways, so you will need to think about how to teach different students. You are likely to use lots of different teaching tools, including <u>podcasts</u>, interactive whiteboards, or equipment such as blocks or tangrams. Teachers sometimes help their students outside of the classroom too. This might mean helping a student after school or at home. Although you will be mostly classroom-based, you may take your students on field trips.

Tangrams

To teach math at a secondary school, you will need a math degree and training as a teacher. You will need to be patient and encouraging and be good at talking to students, parents and caregivers, and colleagues.

ASTRONOMER

Do you ever look at a starry night sky and wonder exactly what is out there and how the universe came to be? If so, astronomy sounds like a great career choice for you.

Astronomers study the planets, stars, and galaxies. Some are observational astronomers. This means they use cameras, <u>satellites,</u> and telescopes to make their observations. Others work as theoretical astronomers. This means that they use mathematical and computer software to investigate and explain what has been recorded. Astronomers try to find out everything about the universe, including how it began and what might happen next.

Astronomical observatory

Astronomers usually work in universities or in specialist <u>research</u> organizations. You might be part of projects that investigate things such as <u>supernovae</u>. Other important parts of an astronomer's work include raising money for your research, showing what you have found at conferences, and working with astronomers in other countries.

Some astronomers think that the star Betelgeuse could be close to dying in a supernova explosion.

There are lots of different roles you could have as an astronomer. You might design telescopes, or you might study how the universe began. Some astronomers research how life on Earth began and whether life may exist on other planets. Other astronomers study photographs and information to work out the history, climate, and landscape of planets and other objects in space. There are also astronomers who look at things collected from space missions, such as rocks from Mars. Some organizations employ astronomers as outreach workers to share knowledge, for example developing education programs for schoolchildren.

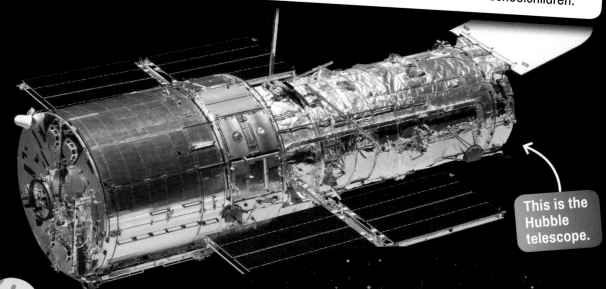

This is the Hubble telescope.

This is the remains of a supernova called the Crab Nebula.

As well as a degree in math, astronomy, physics, or computer science—and possibly a second degree (called a master's degree) too—you'll also need a PhD. This is the highest level of degree. You will also need excellent computer skills.

STATISTICIAN

The work of a statistician is to collect, study, and understand information. Statisticians write reports and give advice to governments or companies about what they should do next.

Many statisticians are employed by governments. Some work for <u>market research companies</u>, hospitals, or universities. Others are employed by environmental organizations, banks, insurance companies, or research organizations. If you work for an environmental agency, for example, you might collect and study data to check air pollution levels.

Government statisticians might look at the need for public services such as education and health. This might involve collecting information on the number of future students and how many schools and teachers are likely to be needed. You could find yourself designing trials to test the effectiveness of new medicines or working out the possible risks from disease outbreaks.

If you work in food production, you might collect information on the number of <u>additives</u> that are put in food. The safety of food additives has to be carefully checked before they are used.

Whatever their role, all statisticians use numbers to solve problems. Some projects last only a few months. Others, such as the planning and building of new high-speed railways, may go on for years. There may be chances to go to other countries to go to conferences and share your research findings with others. Some government statisticians travel abroad for work.

You will need a degree in math, statistics, or economics. A master's degree or PhD is also useful. You will need good math, computer, and problem-solving skills. Statisticians often work in teams, so you will need to be good with people.

BUSINESS CONSULTANT

Business consultants work with business owners to improve their business, by looking at areas such as marketing, IT, and human resources (see page 21). They help business owners to develop a business plan with short- and long-term goals.

Business consultants work in their own office and also on site at the businesses they work for. You could work for large companies or governments. After you have gained enough experience, you might set up a consulting firm of your own, which would mean you have a whole team of business consultants.

Consultancies sometimes specialize in particular areas, for example new and small businesses or staff training and team building. Some consultancies help businesses to be more environmentally friendly. They advise them on the best way to recycle and use renewable energy.

There are different types of business consultant. As an operations consultant, you will try to improve the efficiency of a business. This might involve cutting costs or improving the way goods are produced. Human resources consultants help businesses to hire the right staff and then to train them and develop their skills. As an IT consultant, you will advise business owners how to use IT effectively. You might, for example, help to design a new computer system. Marketing consultants help businesses to find more customers.

Marketing consultants help businesses to use social media to reach their customers.

Business consultants often work as part of a team.

If a career as a business consultant sounds right for you, you will need a degree in math, business, economics, or finance. A master's degree in business is also helpful. You will need leadership skills to guide the company and its employees toward their goals. Great computer and planning skills are also very important.

BANKER

If you think you would enjoy helping people to manage their money, a career in banking could be for you. Banks borrow and lend money. When people borrow money, they have to pay interest. Interest is an extra amount of money that is paid on top of the money you have borrowed. Banks make their money by charging people interest.

Bankers have an important career. They are often involved in some of the biggest decisions that people make in their lives, for example starting a business or buying a home or car.

There are lots of different roles in banking. Retail banking involves dealing with individual customers. You will help them with their everyday banking needs, such as taking money out, saving money, or paying money back.

Corporate bankers give advice about money to businesses. You might, for example, give advice on borrowing money, and you might set up loans for big and small companies.

An investment is an amount of money that is spent on something, with the hope that it will make even more money later. Investment bankers help raise money for big companies or governments. You might, for example, help raise money from people to build a new airport or highway. You could work in an exciting area of banking called mergers, in which separate organizations merge together to form a new joint organization. You could help one business take over another.

Wall Street in New York City is known all over the world for its banking.

11-21 →
WALL ST

1-26 →
BROAD ST

BANK

You will need a degree in finance, business, or economics. Bankers must be honest and act professionally at all times.

CONSTRUCTION INDUSTRY WORKER

The term "construction industry" means the building of new structures. Some construction workers help build homes, factories, hospitals, offices, and other buildings. Other construction workers help build roads, bridges, sewers, and tunnels. There are many different types of construction worker, such as bricklayers, plasterers, electricians, plumbers, and tilers. All of these people use math in their work to understand plans, measurements, and costs. Many are self-employed and use math to keep track of their accounts.

If you think a career in construction is for you, there are many roles, each needing different skills. A construction manager, for example, is responsible for planning a project and working out how much it will cost. If anything goes wrong, it is the construction manager's job to deal with the problem.

Construction industry workers often complete an apprenticeship to gain the training and experience they need.

Many more new homes are needed, so the need for construction workers is high.

Quantity surveyors are in charge of all the costs of a construction project, from the planning stage to completing the structure. They try to cut down on costs as much as possible, while still making sure the project is high quality. They choose the materials needed, working out costs and the amount they need. You will need a degree or training in this subject in order to become a quantity surveyor.

Real estate agents sell buildings and land and need to understand what prices these things sell for. They use this knowledge to suggest the correct price to the seller. They then have discussions with the seller and any interested buyers to get the best possible price. Real estate agents make money by charging the seller a sum of money called a commission, based on how much the building or land sells for.

CRYPTOGRAPHER

You probably use the internet regularly, both at home and at school. You and other members of your family probably use smartphones, laptops, tablets, and computers every day. Maybe you or your family buy things online. But do you ever think about security and about how information about you is protected online?

Encryption is the process of turning ordinary information (called plaintext) into a code that hides its meaning (ciphertext). Decryption is the opposite and means turning ciphertext back into information that can be understood. If you choose cryptography as a career, you will help to protect secret information, such as people's bank account details. You will write new encryption <u>algorithms</u>.

In order to become a cryptographer, you will need a degree in math or computer science. You will also need to be trustworthy, as you will be dealing with important information.

There are many possible roles for cryptographers. You could help businesses to keep their information safe and to solve their security problems. You could find yourself working for banks, writing algorithms that make sure credit cards, bank accounts, and online shopping websites are secure.

Cryptographers also work for the armed forces. They make sure that the military can send messages safely without them being picked up by enemy forces. They also decrypt enemy information. You could work for the police force or for a government department. This might involve studying encrypted data to help solve crimes and be able to find any threats. Some cryptographers are specialists in cybersecurity, which involves protecting computer networks, devices, and programs from attack. These cryptographers look at issues that make software likely to be attacked by other people. They test security systems and come up with ways to make it better.

1011001010
01110010
011001

01 00
11 01

VIDEO GAME PROGRAMMER

Are you good with computers? Do you like playing video games? Do you like the idea of working in the world of gaming? If so, the role of video game programmer could be for you, combining something you love with an exciting and challenging career.

Video game programmers turn the creative ideas of a game designer into a playable game with graphics (pictures) and sound. They do this by writing and testing the code that runs the game and brings it to life. Coding means writing the instructions that tell a computer what to do. These instructions are called programs.

A lot of people want to be a video game programmer. You will need a degree or training in programming. Work experience is also very important. You will also need a good understanding of games.

Most programmers specialize in just one area of gaming. You might work as an audio programmer, linking sound to the action in a game. Weapons or magic usually have sounds that play when they are used, while music can create a mood or act as a warning. If you specialize in graphics, you will create characters, places, and special effects that make the action seem real to the player.

This programmer is testing 3D virtual reality glasses.

You might work as an AI (artificial intelligence) programmer. These programmers create artificial intelligence in characters that are not controlled by the player, such as opponents. AI makes the characters behave in ways that are exciting and believable. Lots of people with different skills are needed to make a video game. You will work as part of a team that will include game designers and artists. Video game programmers are needed all over the world, so there are many chances to work in another country, or to travel abroad to shows and conferences.

MATHEMATICIANS WHO HAVE CHANGED THE WORLD

DAME JOCELYN BELL BURNELL

While working as a research assistant, space scientist, and astronomer, Dame Jocelyn Bell Burnell helped to build a giant telescope. Using this telescope, she discovered pulsars, which are super-dense, spinning, dead stars.

ANNIE EASLEY

Annie Easley was a computer scientist and mathematician. She developed and used computer code to research energy systems. Her work helped launch satellites and space rockets, including the Cassini spacecraft that traveled to Saturn.

CHARLES BABBAGE AND ADA LOVELACE

Charles Babbage, known as the "father of the computer," invented an automatic machine that could find the answers to math sums. Ada Lovelace was a writer and mathematician who worked with Babbage. She was the first person to come up with the idea of programming and is thought of as the first computer programmer.

ALAN TURING

Alan Turing was a mathematician and World War Two code breaker. He helped crack the Enigma code, used by the German military to send encrypted messages. Being able to read the Enigma code helped Britain, and the countries that fought with Britain, win the war much sooner. Turing was also one of the first computer scientists.

GLOSSARY

absorb	take in or soak up
accounts	records of money spent and received
additives	things that can be added to food to make them taste better or last longer
algorithms	processes or sets of rules to be followed by a computer
audits	official inspections of organizations' accounts
aviation	the flying of aircraft
cargo	items carried on ships, including cattle, food, tools, and furniture
degree	a qualification in a specialist subject, often given by a university or college to people usually over the age of 18
economics	having to do with money, making things, and selling things in and between countries
environmental organizations	groups that protect and help the natural world
insurance	a protection against financial loss in which a person pays money to a company that pays their costs if they have an accident or loss
investment companies	companies that invest people's money to make more money
market research companies	companies that talk directly with customers to find out their opinions about products and services
navigation	the process of planning and following a route
pension	an agreement where employees make payments while working, and in return they get payments when they are too old to work
podcasts	digital audio files that can be downloaded to computers or other devices
project management	the planning and organization of a task or project from start to finish
renewable energy	energy from sources that can be replaced, such as tidal or solar energy
research	work, such as experiments, that is carried out to find out new information
satellites	machines sent into space to orbit planets, take photographs, and collect and send information
software	the programs or instructions that tell a computer how to work
statistics	the practice of collecting and analyzing large amounts of data
supernovae	stars that explode, causing them to become extremely bright
taxation	the system by which governments take money from people to spend on services such as education
university professor	someone who teaches at a school that people usually go to when they are 18 or older to learn and do research
witness	a person who has knowledge of something and can give evidence or proof

INDEX

Photo Credits

Images are courtesy of Shutterstock.com. With thanks to Getty Images, Thinkstock Photo and iStockphoto.

2&3 – Best Vector Elements, Alexandr III, DRogatnev, VectorPot, Gurza, vasabii, Red monkey, Bloomicon, VikiVector , thailerderden10, Jane Kelly, ZKH. 4&5 – Rido, Monkey Business Images, Travelerpix, Stokkete, Beresnev. 6&7 – zieusin, Craig Dingle, Angelo Giampiccolo, Nadezda Murmakova, VectorPot, Steinar, notbad. 8&9 – lovelyday12, GaudiLab, create jobs 51, Gurza, leosapiens, 1ZiMa. 10&11 – Marko Poplasen, michaeljung, MakDill, nd3000, Alexzel, Number 86, Yury Velikanov, painterr. 12&13 – kan_chana, Andrey_Popov, Robert Crum, Adam Gregor, A Aleksii. 14&15 – Rawpixel.com, wk1003mike, NadyaEugene, Monkey Business Images, Vector Tradition, Bloomicon. 16&17 – underworld, Arga Firmansyah, Artsiom Petrushenka, NASA images. Red monkey, Panda Vector. 18&19 – pod.shutterstock, Ody_Stocker, Melica, fizkes, Creative Stall, Iconic Bestiary. 20&21 – michaeljung, imacoconut, Monkey Business Images, Pressmaster, Bloomicon, vasabii. 22&23 – Rawpixel.com, Syda Productions, Damien VERRIER, Bloomicon, tikiri, Kriukova Olya. 24&25 – Monkey Business Images, Gordon Ball LRPS, karelnoppe, Monkey Business Images, Sea Owl, Keep Calm and Vector, Faber14. 26&27 – Monkey Business Images, skyNext, Aleksandar Malivuk, Jane Kelly, Titov Nikolai, Macrovector. 28&29 – Gorodenkoff, wavebreakmedia, Andrey_Popov, pickingpok, yudha satia, SkillUp, SofiaV, ILantos, Bloomicon, Dacian G, CHSK. 30 – Launch_of_IYA_2009,_Paris_-_Grygar,_Bell_Burnell.jpg: Astronomical Institute, Academy of Sciences of the Czech Republicderivative work: Anrie / CC BY-SA (https://creativecommons.org/licenses/by-sa/3.0)